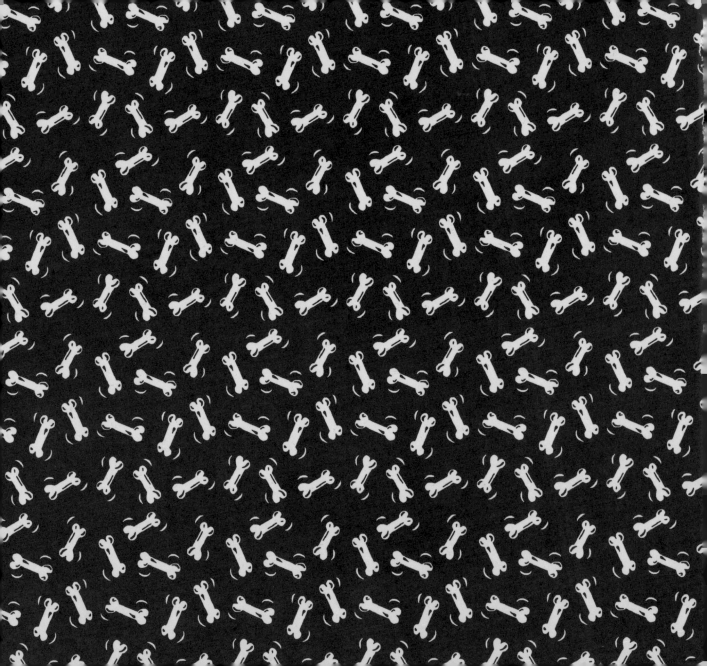

Doggerel

Doggerel

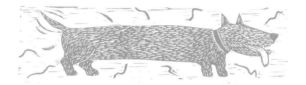

great
poets
on
remarkable
dogs

WITH LINOCUTS BY MARTHA PAULOS

CHRONICLE BOOKS • SAN FRANCISCO

To Huppy Dod, Pinky Pie, Buster, and all the
"good dogs" I have known.

Grateful acknowledgment is made for permission to reprint the fol-
lowing copyrighted works:

An Introduction to Dogs from I'M A STRANGER HERE MYSELF by
Ogden Nash. Copyright 1936, 1938 by Ogden Nash. By
permission of Little, Brown and Company.

The Dollar Dog from DOODLE SOUP by John Ciardi. Copyright ©
1985 by Myra J. Ciardi. Reprinted by permission of Houghton
Mifflin Company.

Verse for a Certain Dog from THE PORTABLE DOROTHY PARKER.
Copyright 1926, renewed © 1954 by Dorothy Parker. Reprinted
by permission of Viking Penguin, a division of Penguin Books
USA, Inc.

Dan from SMOKE AND STEEL by Carl Sandburg, copyright 1920
by Harcourt Brace Jovanovich, Inc., and renewed 1948 by Carl
Sandburg, reprinted by permission of the publisher.

Dog from ENDLESS LIFE by Lawrence Ferlinghetti. Copyright ©
1981 by Lawrence Ferlinghetti. Reprinted by permission of New
Directions Publishing Corporation.

Dog Around the Block from THE FOX OF PEAPACK AND OTHER
POEMS by E.B. White. Copyright 1930, 1958 by E.B. White. First
appeared in *The New Yorker*. Reprinted by permission of
Harper & Row, Publishers, Inc.

Confession of a Glutton from THE LIVES AND TIMES OF ARCHY
AND MEHITABEL by Don Marquis, copyright 1927, 1930, 1933,
1935, 1950 by Doubleday, a division of Bantam, Doubleday,
Dell Publishing Group, Inc. Used by permission of the publisher.

Lone Dog from SONGS TO SAVE A SOUL by Irene Rutherford
McLeod. Copyright 1915 by Irene Rutherford McLeod.
Reprinted by permission of Viking Penguin, a division of
Penguin Books USA, Inc.

The Song of the Mischievous Dog from POEMS OF DYLAN
THOMAS. Copyright 1957 by the Trustees for the Copyrights of
Dylan Thomas. Reprinted by permission of New Directions
Publishing Corporation.

Hope copyright © 1971 by William Dickey. Reprinted from MORE
UNDER SATURN by permission of University Press of New
England.

Jubilate Canis from AT THE EDGE OF THE BODY by Erica Jong.
Copyright © 1979 by Erica Mann Jong. Reprinted by
permission of Henry Holt and Company, Inc.

Of an Ancient Spaniel in Her Fifteenth Year is reprinted from
GENTLEMEN'S RELISH by Christopher Morley, by permission of
W. W. Norton & Company, Inc. Copyright 1950, 1955 by
Christopher Morley. Copyright renewed 1983 by Helen F.
Morley.

Meditatio from PERSONAE by Ezra Pound. Copyright 1926, 1954
by Ezra Pound. Reprinted by permission of New Directions
Publishing Corporation.

For Eli, A Lost Dog by Scott Spencer. Copyright © 1990 by Scott
Spencer. Reprinted by permission of the author.

Your Dog Dies copyright © 1983 by Raymond Carver. Reprinted
from FIRES by permission of Capra Press.

Canis Major from THE POETRY OF ROBERT FROST edited by
Edward Connery Lathem. Copyright 1928, © 1969 by Holt,
Rinehart and Winston, copyright 1936, © 1956 by Robert Frost,
© 1964 by Lesley Frost Ballantine. Reprinted by permission of
Henry Holt and Company, Inc.

Printed in Japan.
ISBN: 0-88701-758-1
Library of Congress Cataloging in Publication Data
available.

Book and cover design: Fly Productions
Distributed in Canada by Raincoast Books
112 East Third Avenue, Vancouver, B.C. V5T 1C8

10 9 8 7 6 5 4 3 2 1

Chronicle Books
275 Fifth Street
San Francisco, CA 94013

CONTENTS

An Introduction to Dogs

The dog is man's best friend.
He has a tail on one end.
Up in front he has teeth.
And four legs underneath.

Dogs like to bark.
They like it best after dark.
They not only frighten prowlers away
But also hold the sandman at bay.

A dog that is indoors
To be let out implores.
You let him out and what then?
He wants back in again.

Dogs display reluctance and wrath
If you try to give them a bath.
They bury bones in hideaways
And half the time they trot sideaways.

They cheer up people who are frowning,
And rescue people who are drowning,
They also track mud on beds,
And chew people's clothes to shreds.

Dogs in the country have fun.
They run and run and run.
But in the city this species
Is dragged around on leashes.

Dogs are upright as a steeple
And much more loyal than people.

The Dollar Dog

A dollar dog is all mixed up.
A bit of this, a bit of that.
We got ours when he was a pup
So small he slept in an old hat.
So small we borrowed a doll's beads
To make him his first collar.
Too small to see how many breeds
We got for just one dollar.
But not at all too small to see
He had an appetite.
An appetite? It seems to me
He ate up everything in sight!

The more he ate, the more we saw.
He got to be as big as two.
The more we saw, the more we knew
We had a genuine drooly-jaw,
Mishmash mongrel, all-around,
Flop-eared, bull-faced, bumble-paw,
Stub-tailed, short-haired, Biscuit Hound.

Verse for a Certain Dog

Such glorious faith as fills your limpid eyes,
    Dear little friend of mine, I never knew.
All-innocent are you, and yet all-wise.
    (For Heaven's sake, stop worrying that shoe!)
You look about, and all you see is fair;
    This mighty globe was made for you alone.
Of all the thunderous ages, you're the heir.
    (Get off the pillow with that dirty bone!)

A skeptic world you face with steady gaze;
    High in young pride you hold your noble head;
Gayly you meet the rush of roaring days.
    (*Must* you eat puppy biscuit on the bed?)

Lancelike your courage, gleaming swift and strong,
    Yours the white rapture of a wingéd soul,
Yours is a spirit like a May-day song.
    (God help you, if you break the goldfish bowl!)

"Whatever is, is good" — your gracious creed.
    You wear your joy of living like a crown.
Love lights your simplest act, your every deed.
    (Drop it, I tell you — put that kitten down!)
You are God's kindliest gift of all — a friend.
    Your shining loyalty unflecked by doubt,
You ask but leave to follow to the end.
    (Couldn't you wait until I took you out?)

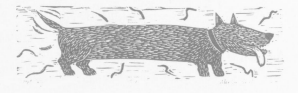

Dan

Early May, after cold rain the sun
baffling cold wind,
Irish setter pup finds a corner near
the cellar door, all sun and no wind,
Cuddling there he crosses forepaws
and lays his skull
Sideways on this pillow, dozing in
a half-sleep,
Browns of hazel nut, mahogany, rosewood,
played off
　　　　　against each other on his paws
　　　　　and head.

ROBERT BURNS

Luath

He was a gash an' faithful tyke
As ever lap a sheugh or dyke.
His honest, sonsie, baws'nt face
Ay gat him friends in ilka place;
His breast was white, his tousie back
Weel clad wi' coat o' glossy black;
His gawsie tail, wi' upward curl,
Hung owre his hurdies wi' a swirl.

† *gash*: wise
lap a sheugh: leap a ditch
sonsie, baws'nt: sweet face with a white stripe
tousie: rumpled
gawsie: handsome
hurdies: hips

Dog

The dog trots freely in the street
and sees reality
and the things he sees
are bigger than himself
and the things he sees
are his reality
Drunks in doorways
Moons on trees
The dog trots freely thru the street
and the things he sees
are smaller than himself
Fish on newsprint
Ants in holes
Chickens in Chinatown windows

their heads a block away
The dog trots freely in the street
and the things he smells
smell something like himself
The dog trots freely in the street
past puddles and babies
cats and cigars
poolrooms and policemen
He doesn't hate cops
He merely has no use for them
and he goes past them
and past the dead cows hung up whole
in front of the San Francisco Meat Market
He would rather eat a tender cow
than a tough policeman
though either might do
And he goes past the Romeo Ravioli Factory
and past Coit's Tower
and past Congressman Doyle of the Unamerican Committee

He's afraid of Coit's Tower
but he's not afraid of Congressman Doyle
although what he hears is very discouraging
very depressing
very absurd
to a sad young dog like himself
to a serious dog like himself
But he has his own free world to live in
His own fleas to eat
He will not be muzzled
Congressman Doyle is just another
fire hydrant
to him
The dog trots freely in the street
and has his own dog's life to live
and to think about
and to reflect upon
touching and tasting and testing everything
investigating everything

without benefit of perjury
a real realist
with a real tale to tell
and a real tail to tell it with
a real live
      barking
           democratic dog
engaged in real
        free enterprise
with something to say
        about ontology
something to say
        about reality
           and how to see it
              and how to hear it
with his head cocked sideways
        at streetcorners
as if he is just about to have
        his picture taken

                        for Victor Records
            listening for
                        His Master's Voice
        and looking
                    like a living questionmark
                            into the
                        great gramophone
                        of puzzling existence
    with its wondrous hollow horn
            which always seems
        just about to spout forth
                            some Victorious answer
                            to everything

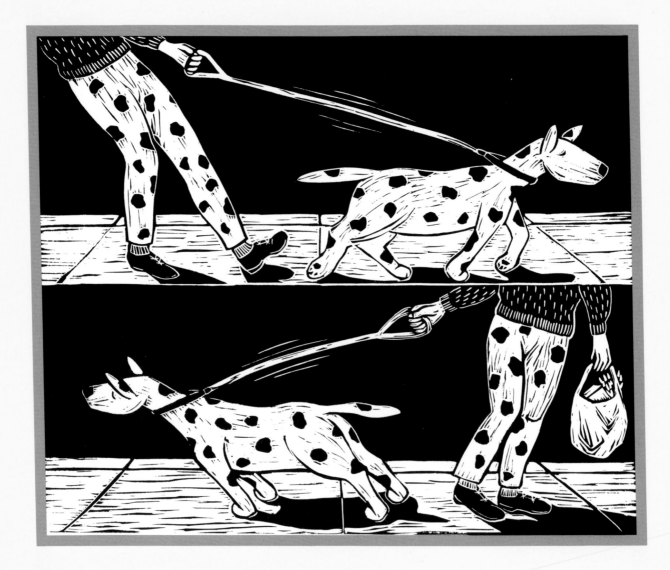

Dog Around the Block

Dog around the block, sniff,
Hydrant sniffing, corner, grating,
Sniffing, always, starting forward,
Backward, dragging, sniffing backward,
Leash at taut, leash at dangle,
Leash in people's feet entangle —
Sniffing dog, apprised of smellings,
Love of life, and fronts of dwellings,
Meeting enemies,
Loving old acquaintance, sniff,
Sniffing hydrant for reminders,
Leg against the wall, raise,

Leaving grating, corner greeting,
Chance for meeting, sniff, meeting,
Meeting, telling, news of smelling,
Nose to tail, tail to nose,
Rigid, careful, pose,
Liking, partly liking, hating,
Then another hydrant, grating,
Leash at taut, leash at dangle,
Tangle, sniff, untangle,
Dog around the block, sniff.

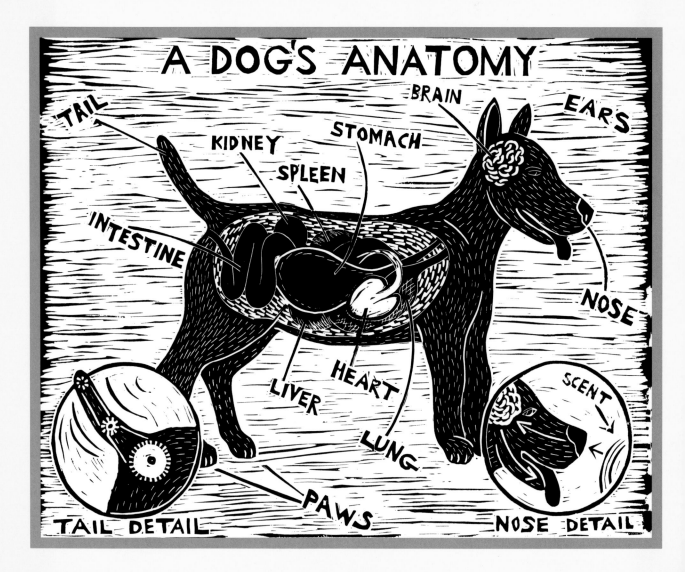

Confession of a Glutton

after i ate my dinner then i ate
part of a shoe
i found some archies by a bathroom pipe
and ate them too
i ate some glue
i ate a bone that had got nice and ripe
six weeks buried in the ground
i ate a little mousie that i found
i ate some sawdust from the cellar floor
it tasted sweet
i ate some outcast meat
and some roach paste by the pantry door
and then the missis had some folks to tea
nice folks who petted me

and so i ate
cakes from a plate
i ate some polish that they use
for boots and shoes
and then i went back to the missis swell tea party
i guess i must have eat too hearty
of something maybe cake
for then came the earthquake
you should have seen the missis face
and when the boss came in she said
no wonder that dog hangs his head
he knows hes in disgrace
i am a well intentioned little pup
but sometimes things come up
to get a little dog in bad
and now i feel so very very sad
but the boss said never mind old scout
time wears disgrace out

† archies: cockroaches

Lone Dog

I'm a lean dog, a keen dog, a wild dog, and lone;
I'm a rough dog, a tough dog, hunting on my own;
I'm a bad dog, a mad dog, teasing silly sheep;
I love to sit and bay the moon, to keep fat souls from sleep.

I'll never be a lap dog, licking dirty feet,
A sleek dog, a meek dog, cringing for my meat,
Not for me the fireside, the well-filled plate,
But shut door, and sharp stone, and cuff and kick and hate.

Not for me the other dogs, running by my side,
Some have run a short while, but none of them would bide.
O mine is still the lone trail, the hard trail, the best,
Wide wind, and wild stars, and hunger of the quest!

The Song of the Mischievous Dog

There are many who say that a dog has his day,
And a cat has a number of lives;
There are others who think that a lobster is pink,
And that bees never work in their hives.
There are fewer, of course, who insist that a horse
Has a horn and two humps on its head,
And a fellow who jests that a mare can build nests
Is as rare as a donkey that's red.
Yet in spite of all this, I have moments of bliss,
For I cherish a passion for bones,
And though doubtful of biscuits, I'm willing to risk it,
And love to chase rabbits and stones.
But my greatest delight is to take a good bite
At a calf that is plump and delicious;
And if I indulge in a bite at a bulge,
Let's hope you won't think me too vicious.

Hope

At the foot of the stairs
my black dog sits;
in his body,
out of his wits.

On the other side
of the shut front door
there's a female dog
he's nervous for.

She's the whole size
of his mind — immense.
Hope ruling him
past sense.

Jubilate Canis
(With apologies to Christopher Smart)

For I will consider my dog Poochkin
(& his long-lost brothers, Chekarf & Dogstoyevsky).
For he is the reincarnation of a great canine poet.
For he barks in meter, & when I leave him alone
his yelps at the door are epic.
For he is white, furry, & resembles a bathmat.
For he sleeps at my feet as I write
& therefore is my greatest critic.
For he follows me into the bathroom
& faithfully pees on paper.
For he is *almost* housebroken.
For he eats the dogfood I give him
but also loves Jarlsburg and Swiss cheese.

For he disdains nothing that reeks —
whether feet or roses.
For to him, all smells are created equal by God —
both turds and perfumes.
For he loves toilet bowls no less than soup bowls.
For by watching him, I have understood democracy.
For by stroking him, I have understood joy.
For he turns his belly toward God
& raises his paws & penis in supplication.
For he hangs his pink tongue out of his mouth
like a festival banner for God.
For though he is male, he has pink nipples on his belly
like the female.
For though he is canine, he is more humane
than most humans.
For when he dreams he mutters in his sleep
like any poet.
For when he wakes he yawns & stretches
& stands on his hind legs to greet me.

For, after he shits, he romps and frolics
with supreme abandon.
For, after he eats, he is more contented
than any human.
For in every room he will find the coolest corner,
& having found it, he has the sense to stay there.
For when I show him my poems,
he eats them.
For an old shoe makes him happier than a Rolls-Royce
makes a rock star.
For he has convinced me of the infinite wisdom
of dog-consciousness.
For, thanks to Poochkin, I praise the Lord
& no longer fear death.
For when my spirit flees my body through my nostrils,
may it sail into the pregnant belly
of a furry bitch,
& may I praise God always
as a dog.

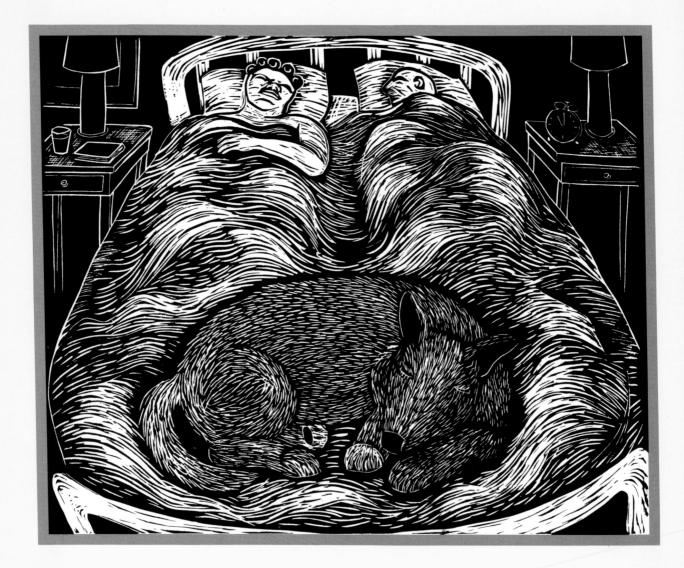

Old Dog Tray

The morn of life is past,
And ev'ning comes at last;
It brings me a dream of a once happy day,
Of merry forms I've seen
Upon the village green,
Sporting with my old dog Tray.
 Old dog Tray's ever faithful;
  Grief cannot drive him away;
 He's gentle, he is kind,
 I'll never, never find
  A better friend than old dog Tray.

The forms I called my own
Have vanish'd one by one,
The lov'd ones, the dear ones have all
 pass'd away;

Their happy smiles have flown,
Their gentle voices gone,
I've nothing left but old dog Tray.
    Old dog Tray's ever faithful;
        Grief cannot drive him away;
    He's gentle, he is kind,
    I'll never, never find
        A better friend than old dog Tray.

When thoughts recall the past,
His eyes are on me cast,
I know that he feels what my breaking
    heart would say;
Although he cannot speak,
I'll vainly, vainly seek
A better friend than old dog Tray.
    Old dog Tray's ever faithful;
        Grief cannot drive him away;
    He's gentle, he is kind,
    I'll never, never find
        A better friend than old dog Tray.

The Woodman's Dog

Shaggy, and lean, and shrewd, with pointed ears
And tail cropped short, half lurcher and half cur —
His dog attends him. Close behind his heel
Now creeps he slow; and now with many a frisk
Wide-scampering, snatches up the drifted snow
With ivory teeth, or plows it with his snout;
Then shakes his powdered coat and barks for joy.

Of an Ancient Spaniel in
Her Fifteenth Year

She was never a dog that had much sense,
Too excitable, too intense,
But she had the cocker's gift of charm.
She never knew what to do with a bone,
But shielded all her life from harm
She cost me several years of my own.

Sweet old pooch! These final years
She rubs white chaps and floating ears
In summersweet suburban loam;
Digs, she thinks, a final home:
Scoops every day fresh graves to lie,

Humble and contented, knowing
Where, any day now, she'll be going —
And so do I.

I said, buying with Christmas care,
Her collar and tag for '49:
This is the last she'll ever wear
(And the same is true of mine).
Equal mercy, and equal dark
Await us both, eternally,
But I was always ready to bark —
And so was she.

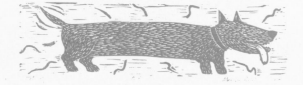

COUNTRY DOG   CITY DOG

Meditatio

When I carefully consider the curious habits of dogs
I am compelled to conclude
That man is the superior animal.

When I consider the curious habits of man
I confess, my friend, I am puzzled.

For Eli, A Lost Dog

I've known grief and, naturally, fear
Yet I never thought you'd disappear
I walked the woods, calling your name
But it must have been obvious, perfectly plain
You were gone, you were missing, vanished, kaput
My venerable friend, my marvelous mutt.

Days dragged by, my heart drowned in dread
Not knowing if you were alive or dead
If some fiend in a truck had grabbed at your collar
And sold you to a lab for maybe a dollar
Or a hundred or a million, really what matter?
My nerves were glass and they started to shatter.

Was it sex, was it meat, what was the chase?
How could you vanish without even a trace?
Were you injured, adopted, trapped, or shot?
Don't you know that without you I'm not entirely Scott?
You were my dogness, my sturdy mixed breed
You were my stupidity, my faith, my great need.

You taught me persistence, you taught me persuasion
You were the key to a complex equation
And now I must if I may abandon all rhythm and rhyme
And send out this message for the ten thousandth time:
LOST DOG/Sixty pound brown and grey terrier mix/chipped left
canine/answers to the name of Eli/Please contact me through the
publisher of this book/GENEROUS REWARD.

Your Dog Dies

it gets run over by a van.
you find it at the side of the road
and bury it.
you feel bad about it.
you feel bad personally,
but you feel bad for your daughter
because it was her pet,
and she loved it so.
she used to croon to it
and let it sleep in her bed.
you write a poem about it.
you call it a poem for your daughter,
about the dog getting run over by a van
and how you looked after it,

took it out into the woods
and buried it deep, deep,
and that poem turns out so good
you're almost glad the little dog
was run over, or else you'd never
have written that good poem.
then you sit down to write
a poem about writing a poem
about the death of that dog,
but while you're writing you
hear a woman scream
your name, your first name,
both syllables,
and your heart stops.
after a minute, you continue writing.
she screams again.
you wonder how long this can go on.

ROBERT FROST

Canis Major

The great Overdog,
That heavenly beast
With a star in one eye,
Gives a leap in the east.

He dances upright
All the way to the west
And never once drops
On his forefeet to rest.

I'm a poor underdog,
But tonight I will bark
With the great Overdog
That romps through the dark.

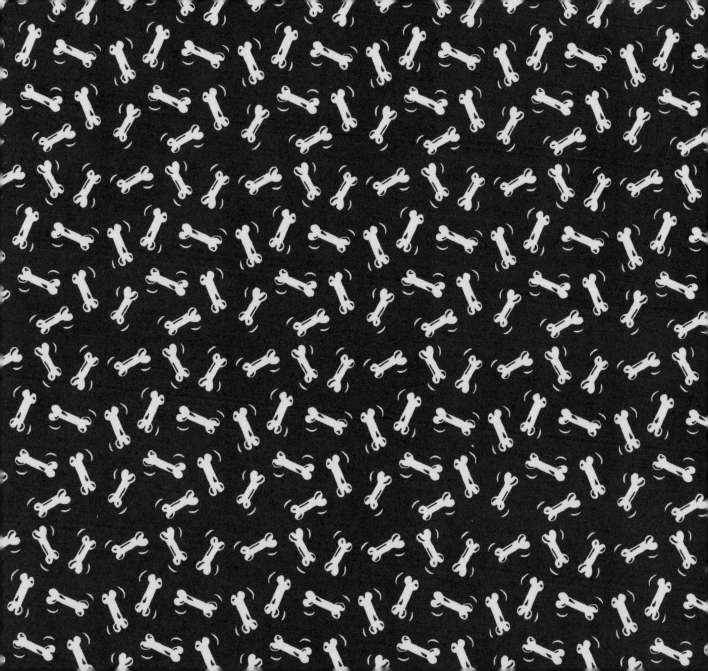